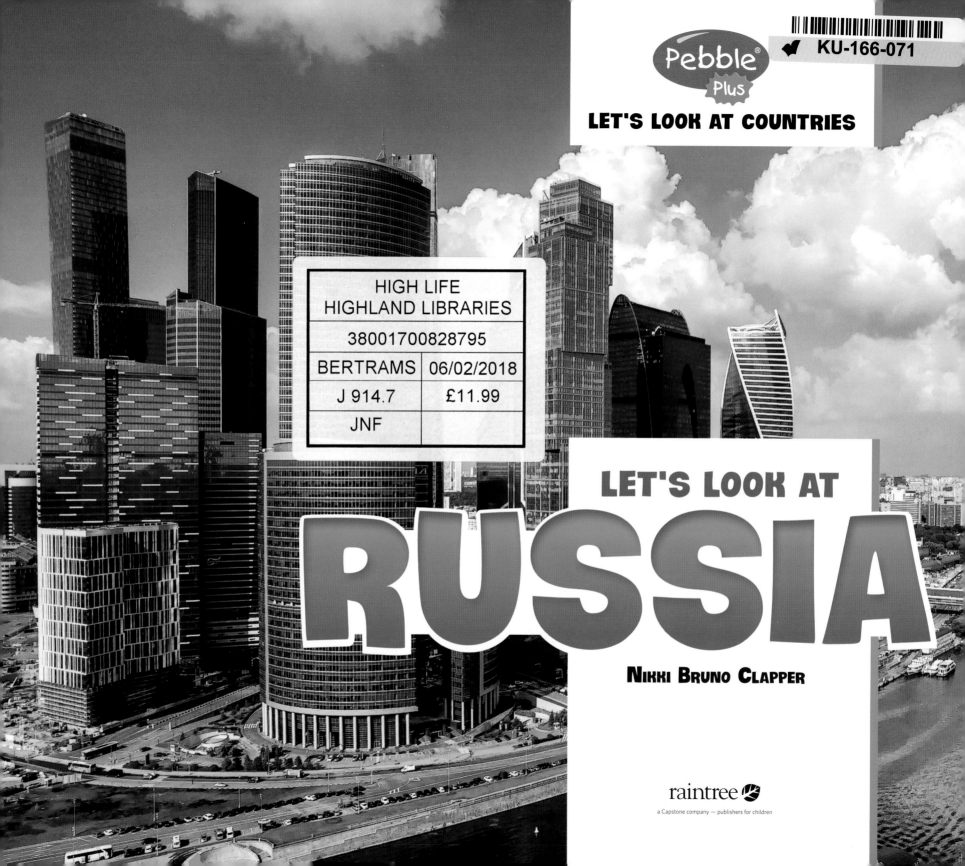

# LET'S LOOK AT RUSSIA

Nikki Bruno Clapper

raintree

a Capstone company — publishers for children

Raintree is an imprint of Capstone Global Library Limited, a company incorporated in England and Wales having its registered office at 264 Banbury Road, Oxford, OX2 7DY – Registered company number: 6695582

www.raintree.co.uk
myorders@raintree.co.uk

Edited by Carrie Sheely
Designed by Juliette Peters
Picture research by Tracy Cummins
Production by Laura Manthe
Originated by Capstone Global Library Limited
Printed and bound in India

ISBN 978 1 4747 5308 1
22  21  20  19  18
10 9 8 7 6 5 4 3 2 1

**British Library Cataloguing in Publication Data**
A full catalogue record for this book is available from the British Library.

**Acknowledgements**
We would like to thank the following for permission to reproduce photographs: Dreamstime: Mengtianhan, 16-17; iStockphoto: Pro-syanov, 13; Shutterstock: Aleksandr Kutskii, 10, Boris Rezvantsev, Cover Bottom, Ekaterina Bykova, 21, EvgenySHCH, 5, Katvic, 9, KUSHELEV IVAN, Cover Top, Martin Mecnarowski, 11, mutee meesa, 22 Top, nale, 4, NaumB, Cover Middle, Cover Back, Nikitin Victor, 6–7, Pavel L Photo and Video, 14, Tatiana Grozetskaya, 3, Timolina, 19, Viacheslav Lopatin, 1, 22–23, 24, vladimir salman, 15

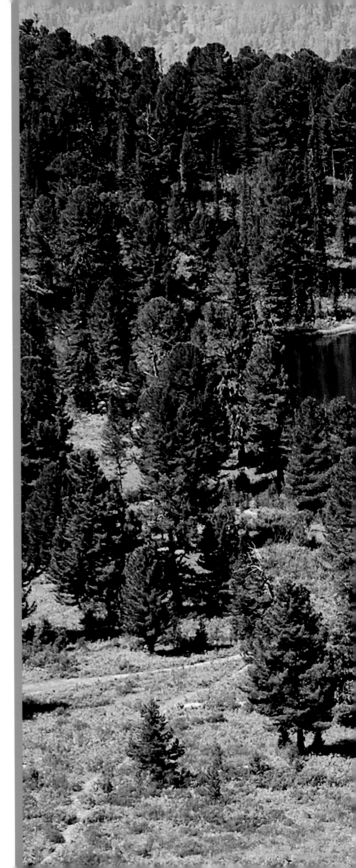

# CONTENTS

# Where is Russia?

Russia is the largest country in the world. It is in Europe and Asia. Russia is almost twice as big as the United States. Its capital is Moscow.

Russia

# From forest to tundra

Forests cover half of Russia.

In the north is frozen tundra.

The Ural Mountains stretch

north to south. Russia also

has plains and marshes.

Russia has thousands of rivers and lakes. Lake Baikal is the world's deepest lake. It is about 1.6 kilometres (1 mile) deep.

# In the wild

Bears and Siberian tigers roam Russian forests. Snow leopards hunt in the mountains. Musk oxen live in the tundra.

musk oxen

Siberian tiger

# People

Many groups of people
live in Russia. Most are Slavic.
Other people include Tatars,
Ukrainians and Bashkirs.

# At work

Many Russians build machines, cars or ships. Others help people. They include nurses, teachers and food servers.

# At the ballet

Russia is famous for ballet. Many great ballet dancers are Russian. Dancers leap and spin. They perform at theatres in big cities.

# At the table

Russians eat a lot of

soup, cabbage and fish.

Borscht is beetroot soup.

It is served with sour cream.

borscht

# A famous site

The Kremlin is a group

of buildings in Moscow.

It includes churches and palaces.

Russia's president lives there.

# QUICK RUSSIA FACTS

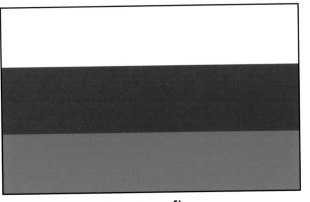

Russian flag

**Name:** Russian Federation

**Capital:** Moscow

**Other major cities:** St. Petersburg, Novosibirsk, Yekaterinburg

**Population:** 142,355,415 (July 2016 estimate)

**Size:** 17,075,400 square km (6,592,850 sq mi)

**Language:** Russian

**Money:** ruble

# GLOSSARY

**ballet** performance that uses dance to tell a story

**capital** city in a country where the government is based

**marsh** area of wet, low land usually covered in grasses and plants

**plain** large, flat area with few trees

**president** highest elected job in a class, business or country

**tundra** cold area of northern Europe, Asia and North America where trees do not grow; the ground stays frozen in the tundra for most of the year

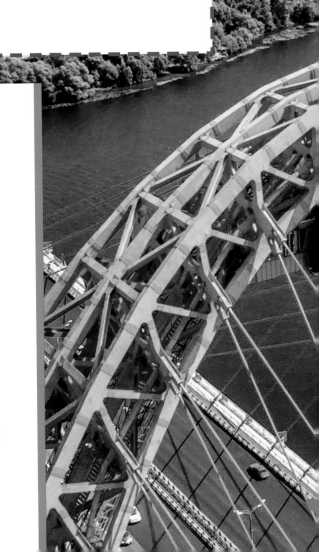

# FIND OUT MORE

## BOOKS

*Russia: A Benjamin Blog and His Inquisitive Dog Guide* (Country Guides, with Benjamin Blog and His Inquisitive Dog), Anita Ganeri (Raintree, 2015)

*Let's Explore Russia* (Let's Explore Countries), Walt K. Moon (Bumba Books, 2017)

*Life in a Tundra* (Biomes Alive!), Kari Schuetz (Bellwether Media, 2016)

## WEBSITES

http://www.natgeokids.com/uk/discover/geography/countries/russia-facts/

Learn about the world's largest country.

http://www.bbc.co.uk/education/clips/zcsdtfr

Listen to music from the famous Russian ballet, *The Nutcracker.*

http://www.bbc.co.uk/nature/life/Siberian_Crane

Learn about a rare bird found only in Russia.

# COMPREHENSION QUESTIONS

1. What types of land does Russia have?

2. Look at the photo on page 10. What features do musk oxen have that might help them live in the cold tundra?

3. Look at the photo on page 21. Why do you think there is a wall around the Kremlin?

# INDEX